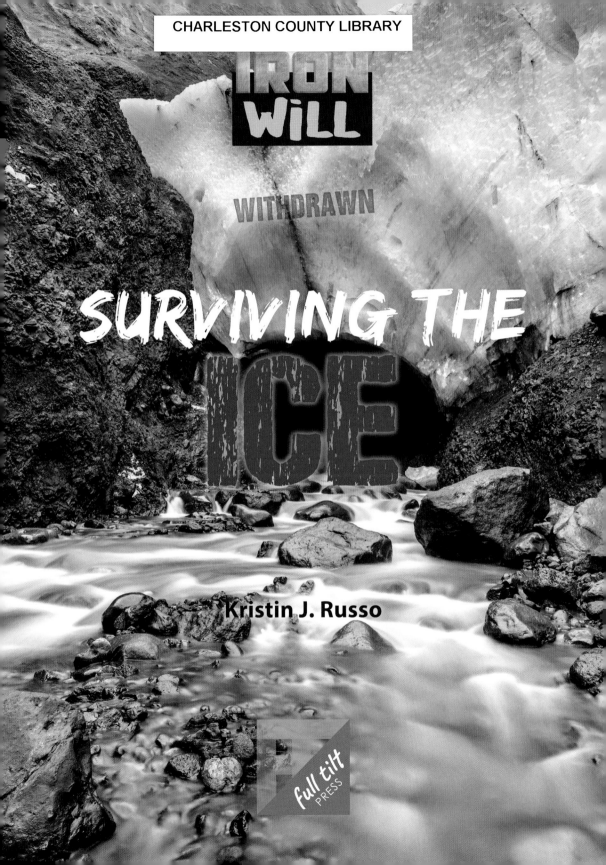

IRON WILL

SURVIVING THE ICE

Kristin J. Russo

full tilt
PRESS

Surviving the Ice
Iron Will

Full Tilt Press
42982 Osgood Road
Fremont, CA 94539
readfulltilt.com

Full Tilt Press publications may be purchased for educational, business, or sales promotional use.

Editorial Credits
Design and layout by Sara Radka
Edited by Lauren Dupuis-Perez
Copyedited by Meghan Gottschall

Image Credits
Getty Images: E+, 11, E+, 45, EyeEm, 36 (sweaters), 36 (tent), Image Source, 36 (compass), iStockphoto,
1, 7, 22, 37 (canned beans), Gumundur Tmasson, cover, Moment, 2, 4, 10, Photographer's Choice RF, 21,
RooM RF, 37 (fire); Newscom: Ken Welsh, 15, Minden/Sergey Gorshkov, 23; Pixabay: BilliTheCat, 39, csharker,
background; Royal Canadian Air Force: 27, 29, 44 (top); Shutterstock: Alexander Lysenko, 17 (Antarctica
map), 35 (bottom), 41, Elena Schweitzer, 3 (top), 9, Eric Isselee, 34, kenary820, 37 (satellite phone); U.S. Air
Force: Staff Sgt. Joshua Turner, 37 (melting snow); Wikimedia: Ansgar Walk, 3 (middle), 25, Frank Hurley, 3
(bottom), 16, 35 (top), National Library of Norway, 31, U.S. Antarctic Program, National Science Foundation,
43, UIG, 33, 44 (bottom), Unknown, 13, 17 (top), 17 (inset map), Wilfrid Laurier University, 19

ISBN: 978-1-62920-804-6 (library binding)
ISBN: 978-1-62920-812-1 (ePub)

CONTENTS

Surviving the Ice..4

Lost in Siberia..6

Tragic Exploration....................................12

Lone Survivor 18

Crash Landing...24

Floating on Ice..30

The Stuff of Survival................................36

Iron Will Stats...38

Map: Coldest Places 40

Iron Will 42

    Quiz 44

    Activity..45

    Glossary 46

    Read More 47

    Internet Sites...47

    Index...48

SURVIVING THE ICE

A hundred years ago, early adventurers wanted to explore the **Arctic** and **Antarctic**. To do so, they had to brave the extreme cold. Many tried to be the first to reach the North and South poles. Some did not make it back alive. Others had frightening tales to tell about the frozen worlds they encountered.

Visiting those places is easier today thanks to those early explorers. But the dangers are still very real. At certain times, it takes less than a minute for exposed skin to freeze in the open air. It can take less than an hour for a person with no shelter to die in the extreme cold. Only those with an **iron will** have any hope for survival.

Arctic: the region around the North Pole

Antarctic: the region around the South Pole

iron will: a strong feeling that you are going to do something and that you will not allow anything to stop you

LOST IN SIBERIA

Egor Tarasov

Siberia, Russia

2016

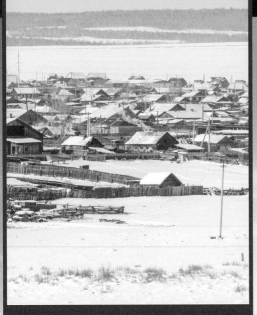

Siberia is 5.1 million square miles (13.1 million sq. kilometers). About 36 million people live in this frozen world.

"A great desire to live, resistance to extreme difficulties, and the belief in a positive outcome."

YSIA NEWS AGENCY, ON EGOR TARASOV

It was a warm September day in 2016 when Egor Tarasov took his boat on the Konkovaya River. He planned to gather firewood along the riverbanks. He needed to deliver the firewood to the next place where he would stop with his reindeer herd. The task was only meant to take one day.

Tarasov is from Yakutia, Russia, near the East Siberian Sea. It is one of the coldest places on Earth. Temperatures in this area of Siberia drop as low as −40° Fahrenheit (−42° Celsius) in winter.

Thirty-five days after Tarasov traveled down the river, he was still lost in the Arctic. Temperatures on the **tundra** dropped and winter storms threatened.

---

tundra: a large, treeless Arctic area where the ground is permanently frozen

LOST IN FOG

Heavy fog rolled in while Tarasov was out on his boat. He lost his way. He ran out of fuel and ate all of his food. He waited on his boat for two days hoping that rescuers would find him. Finally, he decided to walk away from his boat and search for help on foot.

The fog made it hard to see. Sometimes he walked in circles because he couldn't tell where he was going or where he had been. Tarasov ate berries and mushrooms, and drank water from lakes. He walked at night when it was coldest to avoid freezing.

People looking for him found bears on Tarasov's planned path. Wolves had also been seen in the area. Those searching for Tarasov thought he might have been killed. Tarasov had no weapons with him. He walked more than 74.5 miles (120 km) across the tundra. Finally, he found a fishing hut. There was no phone inside, but there was food, and he was able to start a fire. Tarasov learned from the radio that it was October 9. He had been missing for more than a month.

There are four types of wolves that live in Siberia. The tundra wolf eats rodents, fish, and birds. They are very large and can weigh 100 to 125 pounds (45 to 57 kilograms).

SURPRISED FISHERMAN

On October 14, 2016, a fisherman named Dmitry Sleptsov arrived at his fishing hut. He was startled to find Tarasov inside. Sleptsov used a satellite telephone to tell rescuers that he had found Tarasov. Sleptsov put Tarasov in his boat and brought him to a hospital in Chersky.

Tarasov had suffered **frostbite** on his feet. But otherwise, he was healthy. A local news agency reported that Tarasov had "a great desire to live, resistance to extreme difficulties, and the belief in a positive outcome." They said he had a "strength of character." In other words, it was Tarasov's iron will that saved him.

WOLVES IN THE ARCTIC

Wolves that live in the Arctic cannot dig dens in the frozen tundra. Many live in caves or find shelter in rocky slopes. An Arctic wolf mother gives birth to two or three pups per year. These wolves almost never come in contact with humans. They are safe from hunters. Climate change is the biggest threat to Arctic wolves.

frostbite: an injury to the human body caused by extreme cold; typically affects the nose, fingers, or toes

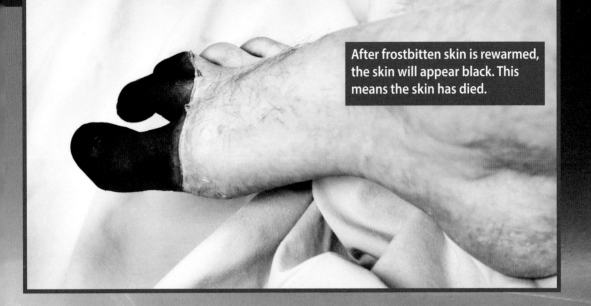

After frostbitten skin is rewarmed, the skin will appear black. This means the skin has died.

RUSSIA

YAKUTIA ☆ ★ CHERSKY

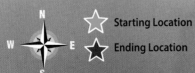

N
W · E
S

☆ Starting Location

★ Ending Location

WHERE HE STARTED
Yakutia, Russia

WHERE HE WAS FOUND
Chersky, Russia

TRAGIC EXPLORATION

Douglas Mawson
Australasian Antarctic
1911

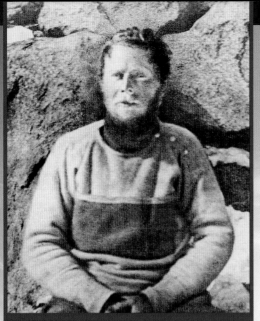

Before his Australasian Antarctic adventure, Douglas Mawson had explored other parts of the Arctic. In 1909, he reached the South Pole.

"I have no hope of making it back alive."

DOUGLAS MAWSON

In December 1911, Douglas Mawson set out with 31 other explorers on a ship called the *Aurora*. They set up three camps in the Australasian Antarctic. Mawson was in charge of the Main Base at Commonwealth Bay.

In November 1912, Mawson and two other explorers, Belgrave Ninnis and Xavier Mertz, left the Main Base. They brought dogs with them to pull their sleds. The group planned to study **glaciers** hundreds of miles away. They had to return to the Main Base by January 15, 1913, or the *Aurora* would sail home without them.

The small team traveled for 310 miles (499 km). Suddenly, Ninnis disappeared into the snow. He had fallen into a hidden **crevasse**. He did not survive the more than 150-foot (45-meter) fall.

glacier: a slow-moving, large body of ice

crevasse: a deep, open crack in the ground, often in ice or a glacier

ALONE AND FREEZING

Mawson and Mertz decided to turn back. They had some warm clothing. They made a tent. But they soon grew hungry. They had no choice but to eat dog meat. Mawson and Mertz both became sick, and Mertz died.

Mawson was now alone. He had very little food. He was more than 100 miles (160 km) away from the Main Base. He wrote in his diary, "I have no hope of making it back alive." But he wanted to live. He wanted to tell people what happened to the friends he lost. This desire gave him the will to keep going. He trekked more than 80 miles (129 km) alone before disaster struck again.

When he was only 20 miles (32 km) from the Main Base, Mawson fell into a crevasse. He was sure he would die. But he remembered a line from a poem by Robert W. Service. "Just have one more try. It's easy to die. It's the keeping on living that's hard."

On February 8, 1913, Mawson arrived back at the Main Base. He was too late. He could see the *Aurora* sailing away without him. He had missed rescue by only five hours.

With no dogs to pull the sleds, Mawson pulled supplies slowly back to Main Base by himself.

LIFE AT MAIN BASE

The Main Base at Commonwealth Bay was well built. Six explorers had decided to stay there to wait for Mawson, Mertz, and Ninnis. When Mawson stumbled into camp, his friends didn't recognize him at first. The extreme cold had given Mawson frostbite. His nose and lips had split open from the cold. Mawson's hair had begun to fall out. The explorers who had stayed were glad when they realized that Mawson had survived.

At the Main Base, Mawson was given warm clothes and food to eat. He contacted his family through telegrams. He spent time writing about his experiences and his discoveries. The next summer, the *Aurora* returned. The remaining explorers were finally able to go home.

When the *Aurora* came back to Main Base to rescue Mawson and the other explorers, the ship was anchored to sea ice while it waited for passengers to board.

REMEMBERING MAWSON'S JOURNEY

Mawson wrote a book about his survival ordeal. It is called *The Home of the Blizzard*. The book was published in 1915. A model of the hut where Mawson and his team lived at the Main Base is on display at the South Australian Museum in Adelaide, Australia. There are more than 100,000 items belonging to Mawson at the museum, including the parka he wore and the knife and sled he used to survive his icy journey.

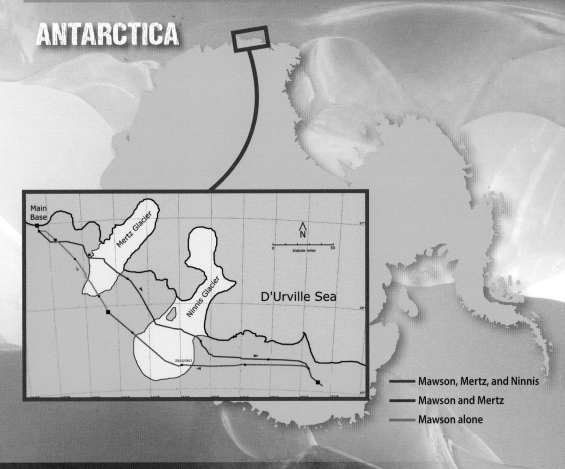

ANTARCTICA

Main Base

Mertz Glacier

Ninnis Glacier

D'Urville Sea

N

0   50

statute miles

23/12/1912

—— Mawson, Mertz, and Ninnis
—— Mawson and Mertz
—— Mawson alone

LONE SURVIVOR

Ada Blackjack
Wrangel Island
1921

Ada Blackjack was born in 1898, in Spruce Creek, Alaska. She was Iñupiat, but was raised by missionaries. She had no training on how to survive in the wilderness.

"... it seems likely she could have lived there another year ..."

CREW MEMBER

OF THE *DONALDSON*

Ada Blackjack was an Iñupiat Native American. She lived in Nome, Alaska. In 1921, Blackjack had a 5-year-old son named Bennett. Bennett was very ill. Blackjack could not afford to take care of him. Explorer Vilhjalmur Stefansson offered Blackjack a job. He would pay her $50 per month to sew clothing and other equipment for a trip to Wrangel Island. Stefansson hoped to claim the island for the United States or Canada. It was originally part of Russia. The job would pay for her son's medicine. She took the job.

On September 9, 1921, Blackjack set sail for Wrangel Island with four other explorers: Allan Crawford, Lorne Knight, Fred Maurer, and Milton Galle. The team survived the first winter. They expected a supply ship early the next summer. But a storm kept the ship from reaching the island. Blackjack and the men were stranded in the Arctic.

ALONE

The team started to panic. They did not have enough food to last a second winter on Wrangel Island. Crawford, Maurer, and Galle decided to search for help. They set out for Siberia hoping to find someone who could help them. They took a dog sled full of supplies.

Blackjack stayed with Knight. Knight was sick with **scurvy**. The little food that Blackjack and Knight had to share did not have enough nutrition. Blackjack took care of Knight, but she could not save him. When Knight died, Blackjack was alone on Wrangel Island.

Blackjack taught herself to hunt while caring for Knight. She trapped foxes and shot birds. She built a platform so she could see polar bears from far off. Polar bears are known to attack humans and Blackjack was afraid. She built a new raft-like boat using animal skin that she used to hunt and fish. She survived for the next two months by the sheer force of her iron will.

---

scurvy: a disease that happens when a person does not have enough Vitamin C

Wrangel Island is located in the Arctic Ocean. Today, there are many abandoned buildings and no permanent residents except for wildlife. Polar bears, arctic foxes, and many types of birds can be found there.

RELIEF

Blackjack was gone almost two years. Finally, on August 20, 1923, a schooner reached Wrangel Island. It was called the *Donaldson*. The *Donaldson*'s crew were relieved to see that at least one member of the **expedition** had survived. A crew member said that Blackjack had "mastered her environment so far that it seems likely she could have lived there another year." However, he continued, "the isolation would have been a dreadful experience." Stefansson did not pay Blackjack as much as he had promised. But the payment was enough to bring her son home. She took him to a hospital in Seattle, Washington. There, his health improved.

THE LAST WOOLLY MAMMOTH

Scientists found bones and teeth that showed that woolly mammoths lived on Wrangel Island until about 4,000 years ago. This meant that they lived about 6,000 years longer on the island than they did on the mainland. There are many reasons scientists believe Wrangel Island mammoths lived longer. They didn't have to compete with mammoths on the continent for food and fresh water. Humans couldn't reach Wrangel Island even thousands of years ago, so the animal was safe from **prehistoric** hunters.

expedition: a journey or voyage undertaken by a group of people to explore or conduct research

prehistoric: something that occurred before people wrote down things that happened

Even in autumn, Blackjack's camp was covered in snow.

✩ Wrangel Island

RUSSIA

CANADA

ALASKA

CRASH LANDING

Sue Hillier
Hercules 130322 Crash
Ellesmere Island, Canada
1991

Ellesmere Island is the most rugged island in the Canadian Arctic. It features large mountains, ice fields, and steep coastline, and is about 500 miles (805 km) from the North Pole.

"I'm not going to leave you."

CAPTAIN JOHN COUCH

On October 30, 1991, Hercules Flight 130322 headed to Alert. Hairdresser Sue Hillier was on board. Alert is a Canadian military outpost on Ellesmere Island. Sue was flying to Alert to cut hair for the service men and women there.

The plane began its landing in the dark. Temperatures had dropped to –4°F (–20°C). There was an estimated **wind chill factor** of –76°F (–60°C). Temperatures like this can freeze a person's skin in less than a minute.

Suddenly, the plane dropped. "My seat ripped out of the plane," Hillier said. "The next thing [I remember] was ice and sliding for what seemed like forever." The plane had crashed into a rocky slope and burst into flames. Hillier was trapped under a chunk of metal. Her pants and boots had been torn off.

---

wind chill factor: the apparent temperature felt on the exposed human body due to a combination of temperature and wind speed

STAYING WARM

Four passengers died right away. Fourteen survivors were left to fight for their lives in the freezing cold. Two could not be moved because it was feared that they had back injuries. Hillier was one of them. The pilot, Captain John Couch, stayed close to Hillier and the other passenger who could not move. He built them makeshift shelters where they lay and built fires to keep them warm. Eleven others, some with broken bones, huddled together in a damaged section of the plane's tail. They shared body warmth inside sleeping bags.

Most of the survival gear that was on the plane—food, blankets, first-aid kits, and small stoves—had been destroyed in the crash. But the survivors were not worried. They thought help was only about an hour away at Alert. But they were wrong. An unexpected blizzard struck. Rescuers could not reach the crash victims from the ground or by air. It would be 30 hours before help arrived.

Wreckage of Hercules Flight 130322's crash showed that the aircraft was totally destroyed.

RESCUE FROM LAND AND SKY

"I'm not going to leave you," Captain John Couch told Hillier. But he could not keep his promise. Couch refused to take warm clothing or a sleeping bag away from any of his passengers. He died from the cold before help could arrive.

Finally, the blizzard cleared. Rescuers parachuted in from the air and arrived in **Go-Tracks** on the ground. Search-and-rescue paratrooper Jim Brown said, "The first guy I found was in pretty bad shape. Frostbitten, fractured knees, frozen left foot, fractured spine, and **hypothermia**."

The 13 survivors were flown by helicopter to Alert. They healed in military hospitals. Their Arctic nightmare was over. Hillier credits Captain John Couch for her survival. "I'll never forget his voice. He saved my life," she said.

A DARK, COLD PLACE

Due to Earth's tilt and rotation, the North Pole faces away from the sun in the winter. It is completely dark for most of every day from October to March. The temperature never rises above freezing during winter. In late March, the sun begins to rise a little bit more each day. In summer, from June to September, the sun doesn't fully set. It is light all day, every day.

Go-Track: a military vehicle with regular wheels at the front for steering and continuous tracks at the back to propel the vehicle and carry most of the load

hypothermia: a dangerous medical condition that occurs when a person loses body heat

Crash victims, including survivor Sue Hillier, were evacuated and flown to Thule, Greenland.

N
W   E
S

☆ Starting Location

★ Crash Location

 Evacuation Location

ELLESMERE
ISLAND

★

GREENLAND

 THULE,
GREENLAND

CANADA

EDMONTON,
ALBERTA, CANADA

☆

FLOATING ON ICE

Ernest Shackleton

Imperial Trans-Atlantic Expedition

Antarctica

1914

When Ernest Shackleton was 16, he joined the merchant navy. It was the beginning of his love for adventure.

British explorer Ernest Shackleton wanted to be the first person to reach the South Pole. But he was too late. Two explorers reached the South Pole before he did. He changed his goal. He decided to be the first person to **trek** 2,000 miles (3,219 km) across the continent of Antarctica by way of the South Pole. Historians call his attempt "a very successful failure."

On the way to Antarctica, Shackleton and his team of 27 explorers became trapped. Their ship, the *Endurance*, got stuck in an **ice floe** in Weddell Sea. No one knew where they were. There was no rescue on the way. Only Shackleton could save his team.

"The only true failure would be not to explore at all."

ERNEST SHACKLETON

---

trek: a long, difficult journey, usually one made by walking

ice floe: a sheet of floating ice

TRAPPED IN ICE

The crew lived aboard the *Endurance* on the ice floe for 10 months. They ate food and used the supplies they had brought with them on the ship. After almost a year, the *Endurance* sank. The crew set up tents and built shelters out of snow on the ice floe. They floated helplessly on the sea.

In the summer, the ice floe began to melt. Then it broke in half. The explorers had to flee. They crowded into three lifeboats and ended up on Elephant Island. There, they set up a new camp. They ate seal and penguin meat to stay alive. After more than 20 months, they were running out of supplies. And they were running out of hope.

Shackleton knew there was no chance of rescue unless he made it happen. He and five crewmembers took a lifeboat and sailed away from Elephant Island. They headed to a whaling camp on South Georgia Island. It was 800 miles (1,287 km) away. Shackleton had no other choice. If he didn't try to reach help, his crew would certainly die.

The *Endurance* finally sank because it was crushed by the ice surrounding it.

THE JOURNEY CONTINUES

Shackleton made a mistake. He and his crew landed on the wrong side of South Georgia Island. They had to cross mountains, glaciers, and fields of snow. Shackleton did not give up. He hoped the whalers would agree to help him rescue his crew.

Finally, he made it to the other side of the island. The whalers agreed to help. They sent a rescue mission to Elephant Island. Shackleton reached his crew on Elephant Island on August 30, 1916. It had been four months since he left his crew. He was very happy to find that they were all still alive. The men had survived for 590 days. Shackleton was never able to reach the South Pole.

CREATURES OF WEDDELL SEA

Weddell Sea is in the Southern Ocean. It is covered almost completely by an ice shelf. This makes it nearly impossible for ships to sail on it. There are myths about mermen with green hair living in Weddell Sea. Seals and many different types of whales do live there. In the mid-1990s, a colony of emperor penguins was discovered living in the Antarctic waters near Snow Hill Island.

The small boat that left Elephant Island on April 24, 1916, could only hold a few people. It had no heat and very little shelter.

SOUTH GEORGIA ISLAND

 Whaling Camp

 Ship Location

 Survivors' Camp

ELEPHANT ISLAND

WEDDELL SEA

ANTARCTICA

THE STUFF OF SURVIVAL

Surviving extreme cold is not easy. Even simple supplies can help people survive while they wait for rescue. These are some of the resources that can help save lives.

SHELTER

A shelter does not have to be big. A tent will do, or a makeshift shelter made from snow or wood. Avoid using metal if possible. It takes heat away and prevents people from staying warm.

CLEAN CLOTHES

Clothes that are dirty or grimy do not insulate well against the cold. At the North and South poles, you need a fresh supply of clean clothing to keep warm.

COMPASS

The landscape in the tundra can look the same for miles and miles. If the fog rolls in, you may lose your sense of direction. A compass will show you magnetic North and keep you on track.

FIRE

The most important thing in the extreme cold is to stay warm. Bring a waterproof fire kit with matches and other materials. Lighting a fire while you wait for rescue will help you stay alive. If you light the fire in your shelter, make sure you have a ventilation hole for the smoke.

FOOD

Nothing grows in the winter months in the Arctic and Antarctic. Even in summer, very little food grows on the tundra. Bring a supply of food that will not spoil. Wild fish and seaweed are also food sources.

SATELLITE PHONE

It is important to be able to call for help in an emergency. A satellite phone can be used in remote places where there is no cell service.

WATER

It is easy to get water at the North and South poles. It is best to melt snow and ice before you drink it to keep your body temperature even. Boil the water or use water purifying tablets to make sure the water is safe to drink.

A strange thing happened to 16 **Danish fishermen** in 1980. After a shipwreck in the North Sea, they spent more than an hour in the freezing cold waters. Then, they were rescued by a nearby ship. They all went below deck for a hot drink. Suddenly, they all dropped dead. Their bodies had **rewarming shock**.

A 2-year-old girl in Saskatchewan, Canada, is the **youngest survivor** of the coldest temperature. In 1994, the girl wandered out of her house on a –8°F (–22°C) night. When she was found, her **core body temperature** was 57°F (14°C). Doctors were able to save her.

In January 1982, **more than 100 deaths** were attributed to a cold wave that swept across the **United States**. People were killed in traffic accidents caused by icy weather. Slick runways caused airplane accidents that injured many passengers. Some people froze to death in their homes.

A United States **submarine** sailed under the frozen polar cap at the North Pole in 1958. Scientists on board the USS *Nautilus* discovered that the North Pole is made up of frozen ice floating on the Arctic Ocean. There is **no land** at the very top of Earth.

Anna Bågenholm of Navik, Norway, holds the record for surviving as an adult with the **lowest body temperature**. She fell into a stream of frigid water in the **Kjolen Mountains** while skiing in May 1999. Doctors who saved her reported that at its lowest, Bågenholm's core temperature reached 56.7°F (13.7°C).

Eight countries exist within the boundaries of the **Arctic Circle**. People who live at the northern tips of Canada, Finland, Greenland, Iceland, Norway, Sweden, Russia, and the United States live inside the Arctic Circle.

Winter 1985 broke records for snowfall and low temperatures. On January 12, a record-breaking **13.2 inches** (33.5 centimeters) of **snow** fell in San Antonio, Texas. On January 21, 1985, it was only 7°F (−14°C) in Washington, D.C. **President Ronald Reagan's** inauguration took place indoors, and the parade was cancelled.

COLDEST PLACES

The coldest places on earth are very extreme. They are not just difficult to survive in; simply existing can be very uncomfortable or even deadly.

1. VOSTOK STATION, ANTARCTICA

Vostok Station on Antarctica is a research post, founded by the Soviet Union (Russia) in 1957. About a dozen people live at the station during the winter. Vostok Station recorded the lowest temperature ever on Earth, at −128.6°F (−89.2°C).

2. EISMITTE, GREENLAND

Eismitte's average overall temperature is −22°C (−30°C). The name *Eismette* means "Ice-Center" in German. In 1930, the area was the site of a famous expedition to study the ice sheet, which is one of the coldest places in the Northern hemisphere. Two people lost their lives.

VIEW OF EARTH'S SOUTH POLE

3. VERKHOYANSK, RUSSIA

Verkhoyansk is near the Arctic Circle. There are about 1,400 people who live there. They don't need refrigerators. It's cold enough to store food in the basements of their homes. Drinking water is delivered as ice blocks that need to be melted.

4. SNAG, YUKON

Snag, Yukon, is the coldest city in Canada. A temperature of –81°F (–62.8°C) was recorded on February 3, 1947. That's the lowest temperature ever recorded in continental North America.

IRON WILL

No one can live at the North Pole. There is no land at the very top of Earth. There is only icy water and ice floes. Even in summer, temperatures at the North Pole average near freezing. But people can and do live at the South Pole. About 4,000 scientists live at research stations in Antarctica in the summer. About 1,000 scientists live at the South Pole during the winter. Today's scientists are just as curious about the Arctic and Antarctica as the adventurers of long ago. And just like the early explorers, today's adventurers must prepare for challenges. They must work together and share an iron will to survive in the world's coldest places.

The Amundsen-Scott Station at the South Pole experiences six months of constant sun, followed by six months of constant darkness. It is the only place on Earth where people live through this phenomena.

QUIZ

1 What did Douglas Mawson write in his diary after two of his crewmates died in the Antarctic?

2 Where was Hercules Flight 130322 headed when it crashed on Ellesmere Island?

3 How many days did Ernest Shackleton's crew survive stranded in the Antarctic?

4 Why can't people live at the North Pole?

5 How many scientists live in Antarctica during the winter?

6 How is drinking water delivered to Verkhoyansk?

ANSWERS

1. "I have no hope of making it back alive."

2. To Alert, a Canadian military post in Nunavut, Canada

3. 590 days

4. Because there is no real land there, only icy water and ice floes.

5. About 4,000

6. As blocks of ice

ACTIVITY

Imagine that you are lost at the South Pole. Create a plan for what you will need to do to survive. Answers these questions:

- How will you create a shelter?
- How will you build a fire to stay warm?
- How will you call for help?

Then, make a list of all the items that you will need.

- Identify the items that can be found in nature in the Arctic or Antarctic.
- Decide what items you will need to bring with you.

Finally, share your plan with your classmates. Ask them to share their ideas with you.

GLOSSARY

Antarctic: the region around the South Pole

Arctic: the region around the North Pole

crevasse: a deep, open crack in the ground, often in ice or a glacier

expedition: a journey or voyage undertaken by a group of people to explore or conduct research

frostbite: an injury to the human body caused by extreme cold; typically affects the nose, fingers, or toes

glacier: a slow-moving, large body of ice

Go-Track: a military vehicle with regular wheels at the front for steering and continuous tracks at the back to propel the vehicle and carry most of the load

hypothermia: a dangerous medical condition that occurs when a person loses body heat

ice floe: a sheet of floating ice

iron will: a strong feeling that you are going to do something and that you will not allow anything to stop you

prehistoric: something that occurred before people wrote down things that happened

scurvy: a disease that happens when a person does not have enough Vitamin C

trek: a long, difficult journey, usually one made by walking

tundra: a large, treeless Arctic area where the ground is permanently frozen

wind chill factor: the apparent temperature felt on the exposed human body due to a combination of temperature and wind speed

READ MORE

O'Brien, Cynthia. *Explore with John Franklin.* New York: Crabtree Publishing Company, 2016.

Rogers, Stan. *Northwest Passage.* Toronto: Groundwood Books/House of Anansi Press, 2013.

Sandler, Martin W. *The Impossible Rescue: The True Story of an Amazing Arctic Adventure.* Somerville, Mass.: Candlewick Press, 2012.

Wallace, Sandra Neil. *Bound by Ice: A True North Pole Survival Story.* Honesdale, Pa.: Calkins Creek, 2017.

West, David. *Ten of the Best Adventures in Frozen Landscapes.* New York: Crabtree Publishing Company, 2016.

INTERNET SITES

https://kids.nationalgeographic.com/explore/nature/habitats/polar/#emperor-penguin-chicks.jpg
Learn how animals live in the extreme cold at the North and South poles.

https://www.cbc.ca/kidscbc2/the-feed/whats-the-story-the-arctic
Explore the Arctic and Antarctic regions. Watch videos and play games!

https://www.activewild.com/the-arctic-facts-for-kids
Learn about the people and wildlife who live in the frigid temperatures of the Arctic Circle.

https://explore.quarkexpeditions.com/blog/the-arctic-through-the-eyes-of-a-9-year-old
Read the adventures of a 9-year-old blogger who traveled to the Arctic Circle with his family.

INDEX

Alaska 19, 23
Antarctic (Antarctica) 5, 12–17, 30–35, 37, 40, 42
Arctic 5, 7, 10, 13, 19, 21, 25, 28, 37, 39, 41, 42

Blackjack, Ada 18–23

Canada (Canadian) 19, 24–29, 38, 39, 41
crevasse 13, 14

frostbite 10, 11, 16, 28

glaciers 13, 17, 34
Greenland 29, 39, 40

Hercules 130322 24–29
hypothermia 28

mammoths 22
Mawson, Douglas 12–17

North Pole 5, 25, 28, 36, 37, 39, 42

penguins 32, 34

Russia 6–11, 19, 23, 39, 40, 41

scurvy 20
Shackleton, Ernest 30–35
shelter 5, 10, 26, 32, 35, 36, 37
South Pole 5, 13, 31, 34, 36, 37, 42, 43

Tarasov, Egor 6–11
tundra 7, 8, 9, 10, 36, 37

wolves 8, 9, 10